I Can Be Anything

I CAN BE A
TEACHER

By Michou Franco

Gareth Stevens
PUBLISHING

Please visit our website, www.garethstevens.com. For a free color catalog of all our high-quality books, call toll free 1-800-542-2595 or fax 1-877-542-2596.

Cataloging-in-Publication Data

Names: Franco, Michou.
Title: I can be a teacher / Michou Franco.
Description: New York : Gareth Stevens Publishing, 2018. | Series: I can be anything! | Includes index.
Identifiers: ISBN 9781482463330 (pbk.) | ISBN 9781482463354 (library bound) | ISBN 9781482463347 (6 pack)
Subjects: LCSH: Teachers–Juvenile literature. | Teaching–Vocational guidance–Juvenile literature.
Classification: LCC LB1775.F73 2018 | DDC 371.102–dc23

First Edition

Published in 2018 by
Gareth Stevens Publishing
111 East 14th Street, Suite 349
New York, NY 10003

Copyright © 2018 Gareth Stevens Publishing

Editor: Therese Shea
Designer: Sarah Liddell

Photo credits: Cover, p. 1 (kid) stockyimages/Shutterstock.com; cover, p. 1 (background) Serhii Fedoruk/Shutterstock.com; cover, p. 1 (chalk) AlexandreNunes/Shutterstock.com; cover, p. 1 (numbers) Tata Sid/Shutterstock.com; pp. 5, 17 Monkey Business Images/Shutterstock.com; p. 7 Minerva Studio/Shutterstock.com; pp. 9, 19 ESB Professional/Shutterstock.com; p. 11 iofoto/Shutterstock.com; p. 13 Tyler Olson/Shutterstock.com; p. 15 2xSamara.com/Shutterstock.com; pp. 21, 24 (coach) bikeriderlondon/Shutterstock.com; p. 23 MelashaCat/Shutterstock.com; p. 24 (soccer) matimix/Shutterstock.com.

Printed in the United States of America

CPSIA compliance information: Batch #CS17GS: For further information contact Gareth Stevens, New York, New York at 1-800-542-2595.

Contents

Teachers help
in so many ways!

Teachers teach us.
Mr. Lee
teaches math.

Teachers read to us. Ms. Green reads us a funny book!

Teachers check our work.
I got an A!

A
Name: David
state door paper
word floor school
apple roof road
house tree city
mouse star mail
table moon stamp
pencil earth street
heart stove police
glass oven sign
A
Name: Georgia
state door paper
word floor school
apple roof road
house tree city
mouse star mail
table moon stamp
pencil earth street
heart stove police
glass oven sign

Teachers make sure
we're safe.
Mrs. Ryan tells us
the school rules.

Teachers take us
on field trips.
We went to the farm!

Teachers listen.
I can talk to my teacher.

Teachers help us have fun, too!

Some teachers
are coaches!
Miss Carr is my
soccer coach.

I can be a teacher.
So can you!

Words to Know

coach

soccer

Index